The Great Treasure Hunt

by
Jim Spillman

True Potential Publishing

Travelers Rest, South Carolina

Published by:
True Potential Publishing
PO Box 904
Travelers Rest, SC 29690
info@tppress.com
http://tppress.com

THE GREAT TREASURE HUNT
Original copyright 1981, Omega Publications
P.O. Box 4130, Medford, OR 97501

ISBN 978-0-9767811-7-2
Library of Congress Control Number: 2006940139
Printed in the United States of America

Dedication

This book is dedicated to the "Children of Israel," and the "Body of Christ"; truly the "household of God." His promises, made from the foundation of time, are not only true, but they are being fulfilled now. What a glorious day for the Child of God!

Rejoice O' Jew and Gentile, "for your redemption draweth nigh."

This printing is dedicated to the memory of James R. Spillman, who walked with God and served Him in life. The evidence of his labor on earth continues to bear fruit in the lives of those he touched.

"Being confident of this very thing, that he which hath begun a good work in you will perform it until the day of Jesus Christ:" Philippians 1:6

Acknowledgement

John Brown of Zion Oil & Gas Company is gratefully acknowledged for his continued faith and dedication to the fulfillment of the promise of oil in Israel.

> *Also concerning the foreigner who is not of thy people Israel, when he comes from a far country for Thy name's sake (for they will hear of Thy great name and Thy mighty hand, and of Thine outstretched arm); when he comes and prays toward this house, hear Thou in heaven Thy dwelling place, and do according to all for which the foreigner calls to Thee, in order that all the peoples of the earth may know Thy name, to fear Thee, as do Thy people Israel, and that they may know that this house which I have built is called by Thy name.*
>
> *I Kings 8: 41 – 43*

Contents

Buried Treasure!

Have you ever dreamed of discovering buried treasure? I have. As a child I read stories such as Treasure Island and dreamt of gold doubloons and the Spanish Main. Step by step I would follow Long John Silver to see if he would find the treasure. There was, of course, a treasure map with its mysterious "X" that marked the spot where the treasure was buried.

The "X" showed you where to dig, but finding the spot marked by the "X" was a succession of riddles. Solving each riddle brought you closer to where the treasure was buried, until finally you were so close you could almost touch it. However, there was one final puzzle to solve which led to the exciting pace-off that stopped at the mysterious "X." The command was given "dig here" and the dirt began to fly! Deeper and deeper the digging — higher and higher the suspense, until you were certain that you could not stand it anymore! But then, the sound of metal striking metal; a few more shovelfuls of dirt — the hunt was over and the treasure was found!

The stories of pirates and buried treasure have mostly been fiction and fantasy. Robert Louis Stevenson's Treasure Island was fiction. My childish imaginings of being with Long John Silver were fantasies of a young boy. The possibility was always there, but the reality never was. Then a most sobering thing happened: I grew up. Adulthood has no place for stories of buried treasure — or does it?

It Doesn't Seem Fair

It was sometime in 1975 that I seriously began to ponder the obvious inequity of the whole Jewish- Arab situation. For many years I had studied about the new state of Israel and her protracted friction and conflict with the allied Arab nations. I researched and learned all that I could about the "all out" wars of 1948 and 1956. The Six Day War of 1967 was followed with an almost obsessive interest. I wanted to know every detail, every fact. Were these current events providing an overlay for Bible prophecy that together might give us some clue about the "last days"? Were those wars preliminary conflicts that somehow might trigger Armageddon?

Then came 1973; the Arab invasion known as the Yom Kippur War. On the morning of October 6th the Syrians on the north and the Egyptians on the south launched a massive synchronized attack on Israel. Israel, not expecting the invasion, was at prayer. It was Yom Kippur, the highest of the holy days, the Day of Atonement. Israel was vulnerable, and the enemy was stronger than ever before. 1948, 1956, and 1967 were Jewish victories. Egypt and Syria vowed that this time it would be different. Both nations had received Russian training and equipment. This time their armies were ready.

They had a vast superiority of combat troops and weapons. The number of tanks alone was overwhelming. No invasion in modern warfare had assembled this many attack tanks. Egypt and Syria had decided to win decisively and finally. There was to be no more Israel.

2

Part of the overall strategy used against Israel at this time was to cut off her oil supplies. Israel, being oil dependent, could not fight a very long war with her oil imports cut off. Because of this strategy against Israel the 1973 oil embargo was put into effect by the Arabs. This embargo controlled the supply of oil to the rest of the world, causing a supply deficit for world demand. You remember those days well, don't you? Oil supplies were short, gasoline lines were long, and prices began to soar. Remember this; it was war strategy against Israel that caused this world wide oil crisis! A new era was ushered in. From this time forth when the Middle East would act, the world would re-act.

Now wait just a minute! What does all this have to do with the "obvious inequity of the whole Jewish-Arab situation"? Let's look at it. From the very first moment that Israel became a state May 14, 1948, they were at war with the Arabs. Israel was outnumbered by as many as 20 to 1 in the field. Even though they were hopelessly outnumbered the Jews were victorious each time.

Somehow this didn't seem to aggravate my sense of fair play. After all didn't God say that He would bring the Jews back to their land in the latter days, and that He would protect them there? It seemed rather Gideon-like for a small number of God's chosen people to put to flight an army of vastly superior numbers!

But 1973 changed all of that for me. Israel needed oil for modern warfare, but she didn't have any and the Arabs had plenty! This just didn't seem fair. "Lord, you distributed the oil to the continents when you 'divided to the nations their inheritance' (Deuteronomy 32:8). You knew and you told us in your prophetic word that Israel would be in this perilous position in these 'last days.' You promised that you yourself would 'seek out' and search for your sheep" (Israel).

> As a shepherd seeketh out his flock in the day that he is among his sheep that are scattered; so will I seek out my sheep, and will deliver them out of all places where they have been scattered in the cloudy and dark day. And I will bring them out from the people, and gather them from the countries, and will bring them to their own land, and feed them upon the mountains of Israel by the rivers, and in all the inhabited places of the country.
>
> Ezekiel 34:12, 13

"Lord, you would not bring the Jews home from 'the nations' in the 'latter days' to be overwhelmed by their enemies. Lord, you also knew of the integral importance of oil for any country in these 'super industrial-techno society' end times." It means: no oil, no economy — no oil, no defense — in short, no oil, no nation. I just don't understand it. "You gave the Arabs oil, but why didn't you give Israel oil too?" It just doesn't seem fair. These were my thoughts, my questions in 1975. There must be an answer somewhere.

Abraham's Covenant

Could there be an answer in Abraham's Covenant? The Lord promised Abraham that he would make of him "a great nation," that he would give him a land, a country that would be for his "seed." Later on God told Moses about this "promised land" and that it would be flowing with milk and honey (Exodus 3:8). Moses was then directed to lead the children of Israel out of Egypt to the Promised Land, which finally he did. God had prepared this special land. He promised it to Abraham's "seed" and they were to possess it.

Moses encamped with the children of Israel at Paran and then sent twelve men secretly into Canaan to "search" it out. The spies returned with giant fruit and the report that indeed the land was flowing with milk and honey (Numbers 13:1–27). They also reported that there were giants in the land and that it was too dangerous to go into the land, "promised" or not. Only a small minority, two, Joshua and Caleb, gave a positive report regarding defeating the giants. Later, when the children of Israel did cross the Jordan and go into the land to possess it, God gave them strength and wisdom to defeat the giants.

Israel faces her giants again today. These giants want "their" land back. But again God has given the Jews the strength and wisdom to stay in the land and develop (possess) it. All of this was part of my confusion in 1975. God promised them a rich land. "He would help them possess it," was His added assurance. Beginning with Abraham and God's covenant with him, we see two focal points: the land and the people. God promised that he would bless and protect the people, and that he would give them the land "for an everlasting possession" flowing with "milk and honey" (Genesis 17:8 and Numbers 13:27).

Riches Underground

This covenant was an unconditional covenant. God said that he would do it, and true to his word of promise, he did it.

The question of the land being rich on top has never been in doubt, but what of the natural resources under the ground? For most of history, agriculture was the basis of economy and livelihood. Land was valued for its surface richness. But since industry and super industry took over the world economy in the twentieth century, the riches under the surface of the land became far more valuable than the fertile soil.

My questions to God continued: "Lord, you know everything. You know what is going to happen before it happens. You knew that these last days were coming. You even spoke of the 'last days' in Genesis. You also knew that oil would be the single most valued commodity during the end times. Why would you have the children of Israel wander over some of the richest oil lands of the Middle East, and direct them to settle on oil poor real estate? It would be different if the land wasn't an 'everlasting possession'. If the Jews were never to return from their first century dispersion and 're-possess' the land in the twentieth century, it might be understandable. But you promised in your Word 600 years before the *Diaspora* that they would return in the 'latter days' and the land would produce even greater riches than before!"[1]

I asked another question: "Petroleum, how did you become so precious, so necessary and

---

[1] Ezekiel 38:6

indispensable, when you were once nothing but grimy sludge?"

From Olive Oil to Petroleum

Oil has been use for various purposes for thousands of years. It is not known just when man began to use vegetable oil. Different plants were used, but olive oil proved to be the most versatile and desirable. It was used as a lubricant, an illuminant, for cooking and in medicine. When the use of oil is mentioned in the Bible, it is usually olive oil that is meant.

Bitumen, petroleum seepage on the surface of the ground, has also been used since man's history began. The Greek historian Herodotus, in the fifth century B.C., described some of its uses and even where to find it.

There isn't much more that would be helpful in our study concerning the ancient use of oil. But the ancient understanding of "what oil was" is cogent to our search. Invariably when "oil" was used it was vegetable oil, mostly olive oil.

Bitumen, when it could be found, was used, but was primitive in its unrefined state, and its uses were limited. The ancient mind never understood it as "oil." The concept of oil springing up from the ground was beyond their imaginings.

The years passed, by the hundreds and then the thousands. Finally, in the 1800's discovery and use of petroleum became a reality. Oil was processed from shale rock in Scotland in 1850. However, it took American ingenuity and expertise to drill the world's first oil well, on August 27, 1859, at Titusville, Pennsylvania. What a timely discovery it was too, as the United States was in the beginnings of the Industrial Revolution – a revolution that would change the world!

I wonder if the first drill-hand (roughneck) there in Titusville knew just how historic he was. This bubbling crude was to change man's welfare and his warfare. Wars could be won and countries lost because of this black grime that he was now wiping from his forehead. The future of the world was on his face!

From Titusville to Opecville

At first, petroleum was used for basic necessities such as fuel, lubricants, illuminants, and certain questionable medical purposes. By the time the new century rolled around (1900) many more uses and users were found. Hundreds of new oil wells were producing, and John D. Rockefeller, leading Standard Oil Company, was well on his way to becoming the "richest man who ever lived."

Standard, as well as others, now began to search the world for new "fields." New strikes were discovered here and there, but none as large or as lucrative as the Middle East oil fields. The first oil strike was in Persia in 1908, and by the beginning of World War II the Middle East would be recognized as the greatest area of oil production in the world. As late as 1970 it could be said that 60% of the known oil reserves in the world were around and under the Persian-Arabian Gulf.

Intense and sophisticated research and technology entered the "oil business" by the end of World War II. More petroleum products were discovered and quickly made available to a waiting public. Fuels, lubricants and illuminants were more refined. Solvents and surfacing materials were developed. Soap, detergents, fertilizers, insecticides, synthetic rubber for tires, man made fibers for clothing, paints, plastics, medicines, and even TNT were placed under the petroleum Christmas tree.

Every year saw not only new products from petroleum, but new users of the products. More wells were drilled, but the thirst for oil was vampiric. The veins of the earth were opened wider and deeper. The jugular in the Middle East was gushing from every incision, trying to quench an insatiable thirst that by the 1970's was demanding 1.5 billion gallons a day! Oil had become the single most important item of international trade.

By 1960, certain oil-exporting countries felt the need of unity and concerted decision and action. In 1960, Saudi Arabia, Iran (Persia), Iraq, and Kuwait joined Venezuela as the charter members of OPEC (The Organization of Petroleum Exporting Countries). Thirty years later there would be many more members of OPEC.

Although demand was outrageous, world supplies were still higher than world demand, and the Saudi production was so high that the market held steady at around $2.00 a barrel all through the 60's. Gasoline was the greatest American bargain. Giant automobiles would guzzle this cheap fuel at 10 times the rate of any other country.

The United States, drunk for so long on cheap gas, was about to experience its first case of the D.T.'s, for a blood feud that had broken out 3,900 years ago was about to break out on its bloodiest, most costly battle yet.

Prayer, Blood and Oil

The autumn of 1973 will go down in history as the "beginning of the end." As the Arabs launched their surprise attack against a truly surprised Israel, forces were being put into motion that would change the world! Aside from the grim reports of casualties and carnage of the intense war effort on Yom Kippur, world political and economic change was also triggered. The international body politic was in seizure.

The Arabs were fighting a *total* war. One of the most important things that they could do to cripple Israel was to cut off her oil supplies and the supply of any nation that aided her. On October 17, 1973, that is exactly what happened. Arab oil producers, in a Kuwait meeting, voted to reduce the output of oil. Some of the Arab states stopped altogether the export of oil to the United States.

The following month, on November 6, the Common Market, completely dependent on the free flow of Arab oil, endorsed a document calling for the Israelis to withdraw from occupied territories.

The United States, Israel's only strong ally, found herself increasingly isolated by world opinion. The other power blocs of the world were pro-Arab. The communist bloc was supplying arms to Syria and Egypt. The Pan-Arabian power bloc and its "diplomatic" tool OPEC were at war with Israel. Europe had spoken through the November 6th EEC statement and couldn't afford to befriend Israel. Japan and the non-aligned industrial nations desperately needed Arab oil. Some nations even felt that the U.S. had been the catalyst to start the Yom Kippur war.

In the summer of 1973, during the debate of the Israel-Arab situation in the United Nations Security Council, the Council had been highly critical of Israel's continued occupation of Arab territory. The Council was moving toward a unanimous vote of censure, only to be stopped by the solitary veto of the United States.

The oil embargo of 1973, which produced a controlled supply of oil, signaled the end of petroleum's supply overage in the world. Demand now exceeded supply. This caused oil prices to double and then quadruple, and that was just the beginning! "Peace" was finally negotiated. The Arabs were richer. Both sides were wiser in the ways of war. Israel had lost world influence.

Arabia, acting in concert, was now a world political power. Yom Kippur had brought a change in the balance of power. The United States and the Arabs were reconciled through the efforts of Henry Kissinger, but from this moment on America would not ever again be quite as "pro-Israel" as she had been. Her heart was in Jerusalem, but her gasoline credit card was lost somewhere in the shifting sands of Arabia.

Later Oil Discoveries

1979-81 brought new petroleum discoveries. There had been new wells drilled, to be sure, but these are not the discoveries to which I am referring. These three years had seen the phenomenal rise of crude oil prices. What was "discovered" is that we can no longer easily afford to buy gasoline for our cars or fuel to heat our homes.

1979 was called the year of crisis in the oil world. Iran was the reason. The overthrow of the Shah and the subsequent political upheaval caused Iran's huge oil production to staunch and then subside almost completely. The United States was hurt severely over this, as ten percent of her oil imports came from Iran.

A check on prices at this time is most revealing. The first quarter of 1979 saw *Arabian light* crude oil selling at $13.34 a barrel. When the revolutionary Iranian students took the American hostages captive on November 4, 1979, *Arabian light* went to $41.00 a barrel – *African light* went to $43.00 (In 1972 this same oil sold for $2.00 a barrel)!

If 1979 was the "year of crisis", 1980 was the "year of surprise". The surprise came in the strange behavior of the oil markets. Experts were not able to tell just what was going to happen or to whom it was going to happen. 1981 saw more of the 1980 surprises. The supply had (temporarily) matched demand, but the prices continued to drift up!

The money flowed rapidly from the West to the Middle East. The Morgan Bank ran several computer scenarios, and every one of them had OPEC with a surplus running into hundreds of billions of dollars, five hundred billion dollars in three years. That's the biggest amount of money ever let loose in the history of the world. All that money and all that oil!

Israel, on the other hand, apparently neither had money nor oil. She was hopelessly outnumbered, she was poor (inflation running over 100%), and she had no oil. She was constantly in danger of national extermination. If only she had oil!

The Great Treasure Hunt

Is there black gold, oil, in Israel? Did God deposit secret riches in the land of promise when He "divided unto the nations their inheritance"? Is that kind of thinking within the character of God? I, for one, believe that it is. Let us read Isaiah 45:3:

> And I will give thee the treasures of darkness,
> and hidden riches of secret places, that thou
> may knowest that I, the Lord, which call thee
> by name, am the God of Israel.

Verse four adds that he is doing this for "Jacob my servant's sake." Are "the treasures of darkness, and hidden riches of secret places" describing great oil deposits hidden deep in the earth? It could very well be, for this Bible text is addressed to Cyrus, not to Israel! Look at the first four verses of Isaiah forty-five:

> Thus saith the Lord to his anointed, to Cyrus,
> whose right hand I have holden, to subdue
> nations before him; and I will loose the loins of
> kings, to open before him the two leaved gates;
> and the gates shall not be shut; I will go before
> thee, and make the crooked places straight: I

will break in pieces the gates of brass, and cut in sunder the bars of iron: And I will give thee the treasures of darkness, and hidden riches of secret places, that thou may knowest that I, the Lord, which call thee by name, am the God of Israel. For Jacob my servant's sake, and Israel mine elect, I have even called thee by thy name: I have summoned thee, though thou hast not known me.

We know that it was this very Cyrus who brought Persia into power in Babylon and then signed the decree of release for the captive Jews. Cyrus founded the Persian Empire. He was unknowingly used of God *"for Jacob my servant's sake."*

But what about *"the treasures of darkness, and hidden riches of secret places"*? Does this mean that Persia had oil under its land? That must be exactly what it means, for it was in Persia in 1908 that the first oil well in the Middle East was drilled.

If God rewarded Cyrus with an oil treasure for *"Jacob my servant's sake,"* would it not be commensurate with his character to bless Jacob in the same manner?

If it is indeed within the character of God to act in this fashion, is it then to be found in the plan of God? In other words, if God would act this way, did he?

The *only* place we can find an answer to that is in the Bible. But where would we start to look? Should we look up "oil" in Strong's Exhaustive Concordance and discover the first use of the word "oil" in the Bible and go from there? No, that wouldn't work at all, for as we have already stated, "oil" in the Bible meant either animal fat or olive oil. No Bible writer or character had the conceptual capacity to imagine oil coming from deep within the bowels of the earth.

If we cannot trace oil by its name *per se* in the Bible, we must then depend on allusion and synonym, on symbol and type. Since this kind of tracing is subsidiary and not primary in its discovery and process, we must seek the primary trace line.

If God did put oil in the sandy bosom of the Promised Land, He had a purpose for doing so. God's purpose would suggest a plan, and if we look hard enough we can discover his plan, and in the process see if there is petroleum present.

Jacob: The Beginning

Although the unconditional covenant of God was given to Abraham, and it was to him that God promised to *"make of thee a great nation,"* we will start with Jacob, his grandson. Jacob was the heir of God's promise to Abraham in every way; that is, what he said to Abraham he said to Jacob.

The greater part of the Abrahamic covenant was futuristic in manifestation. It was in God's plan from the very beginning to use Jacob as a starting point, a national identity. This was clear even before Jacob was born, as he was yet in Rebekah's womb.

> And the children struggled together within her;
> and she said, If it be so, why am I thus? And
> she went to inquire of the Lord. And the Lord
> said unto her, Two nations are within thy
> womb and two manner of people shall be

separated from thy bowels; and the one people shall be stronger than the other people; and the elder shall serve the younger. And when her days to be delivered were fulfilled, behold, there were twins in her womb. And the first came out red, all over like an hairy garment; and they called his name Esau. And after that came his brother out, and his hand took hold on Esau's heel; and his name was called Jacob:…

Genesis 25:22 – 26

The men were as different in their living as they were in their birthing. Esau was rough, an outdoor man. Jacob was smooth, an indoor man. Later Jacob outmaneuvered Esau, both for his birthright and for his father's blessing. The blessing that Isaac gave Jacob, albeit unknowingly, was essentially the same blessing that Abraham his father had given to him, who had in turn received it from God.

Intrigue followed Jacob as he finally got the wife he thought he had bargained for in the beginning. But the wife he loved, Rachel, was barren. Jacob wanted sons more than anything else. Leah, his first wife, the one he didn't even like, bore him a son.

Finally, over a period of years and rather capricious family relationships involving his wives and their handmaids, Jacob ended up with twelve sons. Even Rachel, barren for so long, contributed with numbers eleven and twelve, Joseph and Benjamin. It was a good thing she did too, for without Joseph there would be no future for Israel.

Every Sunday School student knows the story of Joseph and his coat of many colors and his brothers' hatred; how he was sold into Egypt as a slave, but by God's intervention was made the number two man in all of Egypt. Then the famines came in Canaan and drove the children of Israel down to Egypt. Egypt had experienced famine also, but Joseph, under God's direction, had stored more than enough food to last through the famine.

The children of Israel were saved from starvation; Jacob and his sons were happily reunited with Joseph; and once again Jacob and his twelve sons were a unit, a nation in embryo.

Jacob Adopts Two Sons

Things went well for Jacob in Egypt, as the Bible testifies:

> And Israel dwelt in the land of Egypt, in the country of Goshen; and they had possessions therein, and grew and multiplied exceedingly.

> (Genesis 47:27)

All in all, Jacob lived in Egypt seventeen years before his death. As he was near death he called Joseph unto him:

> …and said unto him, If now I have found grace in thy sight, put, I pray thee, thy hand under my thigh, and deal kindly and truly with me; bury me not I pray thee in Egypt. But I will lie with my fathers, and thou shalt carry me out of Egypt, and bury me in their burying place. And he said, I will do as thou hast said. …And Israel bowed himself upon the bed's head.

> Genesis 47: 29 – 31

We must note here that this vow is very significant to the future of Israel as a nation. Joseph vowed that he would not bury his father under the sand of Egypt, but that he would bury him in the Promised Land.

It would have been so easy for the Israelites to stay in Egypt as they were prospering greatly. However, there were greater forces at work here, even this early in the story.

> And it came to pass after these things, that one told Joseph, Behold, thy father is sick; and he took with him his two sons, Manasseh and Ephraim.
>
> Genesis 48:1

Joseph and his two sons went to Jacob's death bed where Jacob had a strange but wonderful surprise waiting for them. First, he blessed Joseph with:

> Behold, I will make thee fruitful, and multiply thee, and I will make of thee a multitude of people; and I will give this land to thy seed after thee for an everlasting possession.
>
> Genesis 48:4

Then came the surprise! Jacob, not even seeing Joseph's two sons (for his eyes were weak), told Joseph that he was going to adopt them as his own. Jacob said:

> And now thy two sons, Ephraim and Manasseh, which were born unto thee in the land of Egypt before I came unto thee into Egypt, are mine; as Reuben and Simeon, they shall be mine.
>
> Genesis 48:5

Why Would Jacob Adopt His Grandsons?

You might ask: "Why would Jacob want to adopt two sons when he already had twelve? Why adopt them when he was dying?" First and foremost, we are convinced that this was the plan of God, and God directed a dying Jacob to do this.

But Jacob's human motivation is clear too. Jacob loved Joseph more than his other sons. He felt partly responsible for Joseph being sold into Egypt as a slave. Lastly, he was so very appreciative of Joseph for saving his family from starvation and then establishing them in Goshen land.

Whatever the motivation was for Jacob's action, the result was dynamic and, as we will see later, strategically important. Ephraim and Manasseh were now to be considered Jacob's sons and would share in the inheritance as full-fledged sons, not once removed grandsons.

As a simple matter of fact, Jacob was giving a double blessing to Joseph by issuing a two-for-one stock dividend! Jacob then put his right hand on Ephraim and his left hand on Manasseh and blessed them. He then turned to Joseph and said:

> Behold, I die; but God shall be with you, and bring you again unto the land of your fathers. Moreover I have given thee one portion above thy brethren, which I took out of the hand of the Amorite with my sword and with bow.
>
> Genesis 48: 21 – 22

In summary, when the children of Israel later would go in to take possession of their promised land,

Joseph would receive two portions with the names of his sons Ephraim and Manasseh affixed to them

Jacob's Last Blessing

As Jacob was now very near death, he called all of his sons together to give out his last blessing. Genesis 49:1 declares this in very interesting fashion:

> And Jacob called unto his sons, and said, Gather yourselves together, that I may tell you that which shall befall you *in the last days!*

(Exclamation mark author's)

Just imagine, Jacob is going to tell his sons what is going to befall them in the *last days*, and he is speaking 1600 years before Christ, almost four millennia before the last days!

Jacob proceeds to deal with each son individually in Chapter 49, but for our purpose we will focus only on Joseph and his blessing. Look with me at Genesis 49:22: "Joseph is a fruitful bough, even a fruitful bough by a well; whose branches run over a wall."

Three things deserve notice in this verse. First, Joseph is to be fruitful. Second, he is a fruitful bough by a well (very interesting). Third, his blessings are so abundant that they *"run over the wall."*

This phrase tells us that indeed this blessing of Joseph's was to be plentiful and abundant. The fruit on the branches would be shared with those on the outside, those beyond the wall. I take this to mean other nations beyond Israel. Still, Joseph's blessing continues.

The Head of Joseph

Blessings? Riches? Could they be the same? Is Joseph to be blessed to the extent that it could be called a national treasure? Has the Bible become an intricate treasure map for wealth that must be discovered in the *last days* (Genesis 49:1)? If so, are there clues right here in this chapter that might help us? Let's press on to Genesis 49:25:

> Even by the God of thy father, who shall help thee; and by the almighty, who shall bless thee with blessings of heaven above, *blessings of the deep that lieth under*, blessings of the breasts, and of the womb:

Most of this verse is self-explanatory, except the phrase: "blessings of the deep that lieth under." What kind of blessing could this be? It says three things: It's a *blessing*, it's *deep*, and it *lieth under*.

The verse by itself doesn't give us a real clue. By itself it is too oblique, too veiled. But we already have two things going for us that we can add to this verse. First, we know what treasure of blessing we are looking for – *oil*. Next, we have the clue in verse 22 that states: "Joseph is a fruitful bough, even a bough by a well."

Let's put our clues together. We are looking for oil, and oil comes from a well. The main reservoir or pool of oil down under the earth might be the *"blessings of the deep that lieth under."* "Too far-fetched," you say? Are we trying to make something fit that doesn't fit? A well could mean a supply of water, or this well could be a symbolic well denoting supply that brings abundance. "It's too hard to even guess what the *'blessings of the deep that lieth under'* means. It really doesn't tell us anything. It is too mysterious."

That is right. I would be the first to agree with that kind of reasoning, and with our initial conclusion. We already know that Joseph's blessing is written in code. It is cryptic and needs a key to unlock it. It was given for those days, but it wasn't to be understood until the time of its fulfillment – the *"last days."* It is evident, however, that these scriptures won't stand by themselves to declare to us, "there is oil in Israel."

Genesis 49:26, the next verse, continues with more of Jacob's blessing for Joseph:

> The blessings of thy father have prevailed above the blessing of my progenitors unto the utmost bound of the everlasting hills: they shall be *on the head of Joseph, and on the crown of the head of him that was separate from his brethren.*

When Jacob declares here that, "The blessings of thy father have prevailed above the blessing of my progenitors," I believe he is referring specifically to Abraham and Isaac. Even though the unconditional covenant of God was first given to Abram (Genesis 12:2-3) and perpetuated through his son Isaac, it was Jacob who received the greater manifestation of the promise.

The covenant is brought into focus in Jacob, named Israel. Jacob's name, Israel, was not only to be the name of the *"great nation"* that God had promised Abram (Genesis 12:2), but Jacob's sons were the tribes, or subsidiary social units, through whom the possessing of the land was to be effected.

22

Indeed, Jacob's blessings did prevail above the blessings of his progenitors even in his own day. But the rest of verse 26 interests us far more in our treasure hunt! Here Jacob speaks of future blessings with, "they shall be" on Joseph's head. He is actually telling us *where* the treasure (blessing) is! Look closely at the words again: "they shall be on the *head of Joseph* and on the *crown of the head of him....*"

This is our first clue as to where the endowment is, rather than what it is. From this moment on we know that the bonanza we seek (oil) is to be found on Joseph's head. God has, in fact, anointed Joseph's head with oil!

But what does that mean? Is it symbolic or cryptic or both? We know it can't be literal. I personally think that it is mostly cryptic. I feel it is only symbolic in the general sense in the meaning of anointing the head with oil.

The Old Testament gives us several instances of this rite. Its usual meaning was to signify authority and blessing being conferred by a higher power. That is what I believe we see here. God is blessing Israel through this anointing of Joseph. However, our goal is not to discover veiled general meanings, but to find specific hidden treasure.

So then, if we can rely on the assumption that Genesis 49:26 tells us where the treasure is, what do we do now? It is clear that the verse is cryptic; that is, it is in code. We must unlock the meaning. To do this we must go on to see where this and the other two clues lead us.

We must follow the scripture until it reveals to us its hidden meaning. We do have a couple of guides that we can follow personally with our clues. Our guides are named Joseph and Israel: Joseph the family and Israel the land. At this juncture Joseph is our guide.

Keeping Joseph in Sight

Armed with our three little clues, let us hurry on to follow Joseph after the death of his father Jacob. Genesis 50: 22–26 gives us the scriptural story of what happened:

> And Joseph dwelt in Egypt, he, and his father's house: and Joseph lived an hundred and ten years. And Joseph saw Ephraim's children of the third generation: the children also of Machir the son on Manasseh were brought up on Joseph's knees. And Joseph said unto his brethren, I die: and God will surely visit you, and bring you out of this land unto the land which he sware to Abraham, to Isaac, and to Jacob. And Joseph took an oath of the children of Israel, saying, God will surely visit you, and ye shall carry up my bones from hence. So Joseph died, being an hundred and ten years old: and they embalmed him, and he was put in a coffin in Egypt.

And so our guide, so quickly followed, is so quickly gone. We must, of course, follow his sons and their sons as we move ever closer to the mysterious "blessings" treasure.

But before we grab our biblical spade to dig up another clue, let us consider the importance of Joseph's

24

life from God's perspective. Perhaps we will then be better able to understand the unique role of Joseph in all of this.

Joseph Left a Heritage

Joseph had gone from prisoner to Prime Minister in Egypt. It was strictly providential that Joseph be in this high position at the time of famine so that his people might be preserved.

Yet, we see another strategy of a provident God in getting the Israelites to leave Canaan at that time. They had to have the time and the opportunity to develop a national strength, so that when they took possession of the land they might have the sections properly allotted to the tribes, and thus prevent the tribes as tribes from becoming disintegrated by settling in different parts of the country. It was most important that the tribes be kept together and be properly located (more on this later).

It was also necessary that the Israelites be taken out of Canaan so that they would not mingle and intermarry with the idolatrous races of the people who also dwelled in Canaan. The famine forced them out of Canaan into Egypt where they were put in a separate place called Goshen.

The Hyksos nation had conquered Egypt before this time, and so there was a Hyksos Pharaoh on the throne during Joseph's sojourn there. The importance of this lies in the fact that the Egyptians hated the Hyksos and would have nothing more than was absolutely necessary to do with them.

Joseph, a foreigner, was favored by the Hyksos Pharaoh, a foreigner to the Egyptians, and so the idolatrous Egyptians rejected him and his people out of hand. This preserved the children of Israel from associating with them and their paganism. This Egyptian experience was also a fulfillment of prophecy that was given to Abram.

> And he said unto Abram, Know of a surety that thy seed shall be a stranger in a land that is not theirs, and shall serve them; and they shall afflict them four hundred years.
>
> Genesis 15:13

He also promised in verse 14 that "afterward shall they come out with great substance."

Joseph's life was integral in its purity and its power to the preservation, development, and preparation of Israel relative to the possession of the Promised Land. It is because of this, I believe, that God allotted a double portion of land in Canaan to Joseph, and anointed Joseph's head with the oil of blessing and prosperity.

Recapping the Clues

Let us now briefly recap our "clue" scriptures to bring us up to date and prepare us for the next step toward the mysterious "X" on our treasure map. First we have Genesis 49:22 that tells us that "Joseph is a fruitful bough...by a *well*." Could this possibly allude to a fountain of oil that would some day spring up out of Joseph's land?

26

Second, Genesis 49:25 speaks of the "blessings of the deep that lieth under..." Is the *"deep that lieth under"* a great pool of petroleum?

Third, Genesis 49:26 points us to the place of Joseph's blessings. It says that they will be found "...on the *head* of Joseph, and on the *crown* of the head of him that was separate from his brethren." This makes it simple, yet hard. We have discovered the place of Joseph's blessings, the top of his head. Now all we have to do is find his head!

At this moment you may be mumbling, "This is ridiculous; this sounds like some mad, mad, mad world television script – long on fantasy and nonsense, but short on fact." I couldn't agree more, for that is exactly what I said!

One of my biggest problems was this: Is it sensible to think that an ancient civilization would actually write something in code that would not be decoded until modern time? The idea was so remote, but then I thought of the Rosetta Stone.

Consider the Rosetta Stone

Ancient Egypt wrote special messages that were carved in stone. The pyramids of famous Pharaohs provide numerous examples. The cryptic writings are called hieroglyphics (temple writings). Hieroglyphics guarded the treasure of ancient Egypt for millenniums. Not until the key was discovered was the great treasure house opened.

It was 1799 that the key, the Rosetta Stone, was accidentally found. It was someone in Napoleon's invading French army who uncovered the great basalt rock. It was found at the Rosetta mouth of the great Nile River, hence its name.

There was a Greek inscription on the Rosetta Stone, and it was this writing that gave the key to the French scholar Champollion who deciphered the Egyptian hieroglyphics. It was so easy to unlock the treasures of millennia *after* the key had been found and applied.

If the ancient Egyptians used the principles of coded language for their own veiled purpose, couldn't God use the same principle (at about the same time in history) for his own purpose? If the Egyptian hieroglyphic key, the Rosetta Stone, was not presented publicly until the 1800's, is it too hard for us to imagine the discovery and presentation of the key to this Bible code in the 1900's?

Remember what Jacob said to his sons at the time that he called them together to give them his final blessing: "Gather yourselves together, that I may tell you that which shall befall you in the last days" (Genesis 49:1).

"Israel Have I Loved!"

It is time for us to give our guide Joseph a brief rest, and follow for a while our second guide, Israel the nation. We remember that Jacob (Israel) made his son Joseph vow that he wouldn't bury him in Egypt, and Joseph, true to his vow, took his father's body back to

Canaan and buried him at Machpelah with his father and mother, and grandfather and grandmother.

When it was time for Joseph to die, he demanded an oath also. Joseph's oath was not with one of his sons, but was with the "children of Israel" (Genesis 50:25). He knew that God was going to allow the children of Israel to stay in Egypt only for a prescribed time. When the fullness of time would come, they would leave Egypt and possess Canaan. Joseph, unlike Jacob, was content to have his bones remain in Egypt until that time. Joseph made the Israelites promise that when God did *"visit"* Egypt to direct them to Canaan, they would take his bones with them that he might also rest with his fathers. The stage is now set for the *"Exodus."*

> And Joseph died, and all his brethren, and all that generation. And the children of Israel were fruitful, and increased abundantly, and multiplied, and waxed exceeding mighty; and the land was filled with them. Now there arose up a new king over Egypt, which knew not Joseph. And he said unto his people, Behold, the people of the children of Israel are more and mightier than we: Come on, let us deal wisely with them; lest they multiply, and it come to pass, that, when there falleth out any war, they join also unto our enemies, and fight against us, and so get them up out of the land.
>
> Exodus 1:6 - 10

From Egypt to the Jordan

The 400 years of Israel's sojourn were almost accomplished. Jacob's family, which had come into Egypt as seventy souls, weak and needy, was now ready to leave as a strong tribal nation.

Moses was born, grew strong, and was schooled by the God of Abraham, Isaac, and Jacob for the arduous task that lay before him. If Joseph, the last great leader of the children of Israel, was the preserver, Moses, the next great leader, was the deliverer. He brought them out of Egypt, through years of futile wandering, to the turbulent Jordan, the river of no return. Moses, now 120 years old, had almost finished his heavenly assignment. He must now pass on the tribal blessings, given hundreds of years ago by Jacob, to the twelve tribes of Israel. It was now time to commission Joshua to lead the tribes in the invasion of Canaan and possess Jacob's inheritance. The land, the tribal blessings; each was dependent on the other.

Once again it is time for us to look closely at our treasure map. We are closer than ever to the mysterious "X" and the richest buried treasure in the history of the world!

The Song of Moses

Scripturally our treasure story picks up again in Deuteronomy chapter 32. This chapter gives us the song of Moses, his swan song, if you please. It was given to all the people for edification and warning. It was his last great sermon. He was, even now, passing the baton of responsibility and authority to Joshua, the next great leader of Israel. For our purposes let us direct our attention to Deuteronomy 32:8-13:

> When the Most High divided to the nations their inheritance, when he separated the sons of Adam, he set the bounds of the people according to the number of the children of Israel, For the Lord's portion is his people; Jacob is the lot of his inheritance. He found him in a desert land, and in the waste howling wilderness; he led him about, he instructed him, he kept him as the apple of his eye. As an eagle stirreth up her nest, fluttereth over her young, spreadeth abroad her wings, taketh them, beareth them on her wings: So the Lord alone did lead him, and there was no strange god with him. He made him ride on the high places of the earth, that he might eat the increase of the fields; and he made him to suck honey out of the rock, and *oil out of the flinty rock:*

The Inheritance of the Nations

The opening statement in verse eight is one of the most dramatic statements in scripture: "When the Most High divided to the nations their inheritance..." As our imagination releases and our thoughts run free, two questions leap forth. *When* did the Most High divide to the nations their inheritance? *What* is a nation's inheritance?

Let's consider the second question first. *What* is a nation's inheritance? I am convinced that it is its land, both the richness of its topsoil, and the wealth deposited deep under the soil. All physical wealth (or inheritance) must come from the land in some form or other, so it seems logical to conclude that the inheritance is the land.

It could be argued, I suppose, that people are a nation's inheritance, but this doesn't seem to be very logical. An inheritance is something of value passed on from one generation to another. People do not inherit people. Children don't inherit parents, but rather what the parents possess.

It might also be said that the inheritance of a nation might be a spiritual thing, but this, too, seems unreasonable. God told Moses that He was "I am," not "I was" or "I will be." Each generation and each person of a generation has the responsibility of personally relating to a personal God who dwells in his fullness in that generation. In the Bible some generations are called "sinful"; none are called "righteous." Spiritual kinship is a personal "now," not a national "then."

My conclusion is that a nation's inheritance is its land, or more specifically, its natural resources. In Bible times, during the history of both Testaments, usable natural resources were either on the surface or close to the surface of the land. Some of those resources were lakes, rivers, shallow wells, fertile soil, trees, and even minerals from shallow mines.

The very thought of something valuable being extricated from deep within the earth, such as "the deep that lieth under," was beyond conception. There were no tools, no technological capacity available for such a project. As we have discussed, this technology didn't come until the end of the nineteenth century.

Yet, if the "deep that lieth under" is oil, this kind of chronological timetable would fit perfectly. Remember what Jacob said in Genesis 49:1? He gathered his sons together to tell them what would befall them "in the last days." These are the *"last days."* So time wise, the fit is a good one.

When Was This Inheritance Given?

Now let us consider the first question. *"When* did the Most High divide to the nations their inheritance?" Long before Adam was created God was at work in the physical creation. If we count back through the generations of Adam to the time of Adam's creation we end up *circa* 4,000 – 5,000 years before the birth of Christ.

We know that the world is much older than that. In fact, there is evidence that a pre-Adam people existed. We know, by countless fossils, that huge mammals roamed the earth. These animals have been extinct at least for the duration of written history.

We know, too, that huge vegetation forests were located in various parts of the world during this pre-history period. But at some moment long ago in the ether-like past of pre-Adam, there was a great cataclysm, a general chaos. I believe that not only did it happen that way, but that it happened as a direct result of Lucifer being cast down from his exalted place in the heavens to the earth. He was condemned to live on this planet until the time of his ultimate judgment.

I am convinced that planet earth came under the scope and span of this judgment, and a catastrophic upheaval of cosmic proportions was set into motion. How long this lasted isn't even guessable, but when it was finished much of the earth was inside-out. In places, what had been surface was deeply submerged. Great forests, gigantic swamps, giant animals innumerable were volcanically plowed under. What had been formed was now without form. What was alive was now dead. For "the earth was without form, and void, and darkness was upon the face of the deep" (Genesis 1:2).

It seems feasible to think that between Genesis 1:1 and 1:2 there was a chaotic period, this very period that we have just described. Verse one says that: "In the beginning God created the heaven and the earth." Verse two continues with the dark statement that the earth was "without form, and void."

As God could not create an earth "without form, and void"; then something disruptive, something chaotic must have happened between the first and second verses. This could explain the dinosaur fossils, the mountain ranges, the ocean troughs, the earth rifts, the tectonic plates, and the huge lakes of highly compressed animal and vegetable matter couched deep in the earth that we now call petroleum.

Jacob is the Center

Returning now to Deuteronomy 32:8 – 13, let's look at verse nine. In the last part of the verse Moses tells us that, "Jacob Is lot of his inheritance." For us, the name Jacob is important here because it was with Jacob that we found our first clues, oblique as they were. Moses, in his death song, almost half a millennium after Jacob, is referring back to Jacob, and to the subject of Jacob's blessing for his sons.

Later we will see how Moses actually passes the blessings of Jacob along to the tribes, even expanding the meaning and value of them. Suffice for us now to see that Moses is discussing Jacob. In verses 9 - 12 he speaks of his special relationship with God; while in verse 13 he gives us our long-awaited next clue, and it is a dandy! Look closely at the last half of verse 13, "...and he made him to *suck* honey out of the rock, and oil out of the *flinty rock.*"

Sucking Oil!

Oil! Could it mean olive oil, the only oil known to Moses? No, of course not! It would be absurd to speak of sucking oil out of a certain type of rock when everyone there knew that oil came from crushed olives.

Someone might question here: "Isn't it just as absurd to think of sucking honey out of a rock when everyone knew honey came from beehives?" The answer to that is "yes, it is just as absurd," but it doesn't mean "bee honey"; it means "earth" honey, a synonym for petroleum.

What we have here is a Hebrew parallelism, common in the Bible. Here, honey and oil mean the same thing! The first is symbolic; the second is literal. A simple way to prove this is to locate the verb of the object honey, and of the object oil. Notice that there is one verb, suck, for both objects. Of course, neither honey nor olive oil was sucked into use.

Even more interesting is the observation that if you wanted to use the word pump in this context, that the Hebrew word here translated suck, is the word that you would use. "Oil out of the flinty rock," remained a phrase of mystery for thousands of years, that is, until 1850, when a process was developed for extracting oil out of shale (flinty rock?).

So Moses, in his song to the nation Israel, gives us the clearest, the strongest clue yet, in our search for this *buried treasure*. Ah, the Bible, what a treasure map it is! But wait, we mustn't get too excited yet. The best is yet to come. We must resume our search for the mysterious "X," for it is there that we will dig (drill) for the treasure.

Moses' Blessing

Deuteronomy 33 is the chapter detailing the blessing of Jacob given by Moses. It is here that we shall finally discover our mysterious "X."

Verse one is our scriptural first step: "And this is the blessing, wherewith Moses the man of God blessed the children of Israel before his death." This *"blessing,"* this Godly inheritance, is the same blessing given by Jacob just before his death hundreds of years before. It was part and parcel of the covenant made by God with Abram two generations before Jacob.

Jacob's blessing was much more definitive than Abraham's covenant, and now Moses' blessing is much more definitive and precise than was Jacob's. In other words, God didn't give all the information to Abraham or to Jacob, but rather gave as much as was needed at the time. Now, as the children of Israel are actually about to go over Jordan and into the land, he is giving a broader and deeper explanation of the tribal inheritance.

This progressive giving of illumination and knowledge is easier for us to understand when we know that the land is the people's inheritance. For the children of Israel this was graphically true. The closer they got to the land the more they needed to know about its possession, its purpose and its properties.

Deuteronomy 33:6 is where the personal blessing begins. As Reuben is the eldest, it starts with him. Verse seven tells us of Judah's blessing, and verse eight begins the explanation of the blessing of Levi. However, those three tribes are not cogent to our study, so we must nod in recognition and resolutely press on past them.

We are about to come upon some very unique and interesting details of our treasure map. The first one is so unobtrusive, so left-handed, that it might go unnoticed by even a careful reader. Let's look at Benjamin, the baby, the youngest of Jacob's brood.

Between His Shoulders?

And of Benjamin he said, The beloved of the Lord shall dwell in safety by him; and the Lord shall cover him all day long, and he shall dwell between his shoulders.

Deuteronomy 33:12

Actually there are only two cryptic phrases in this verse; the rest of the verse is easily understood. The first phrase that catches our attention and makes us question is "…and the Lord shall cover him all the day long…" What does that mean? Is it symbolic or is it cryptic? Is it symbolic, as is the use of *"cover"* in Psalm 91:4: "He shall cover thee with his feathers, and under his wings shalt thou trust..."? I don't think that it is symbolic. I believe that it is both cryptic and literal. This position cannot be proven by verse twelve itself, but we will find that the context of the chapter will provide enough evidence. Sufficient here to state that *"to cover"* means to put something over the top of something or someone. It sounds like rather a childish explanation, doesn't it? Yet, we will see that it will be more cryptic than pedantic.

The questions continue. What in the realm of common sense or imagination does it mean when it states in verse twelve that "…he shall dwell between his shoulders"? Between *whose* shoulders will Benjamin be dwelling? The previous phrase says "…and the Lord shall cover him all the day long…" Should we use grammatical assumption and conclude that Benjamin is to dwell between the Lord's shoulders?

This would be very hard to deal with. It's not difficult for us to understand the symbolism of "the hand of the Lord" or "the voice of the Lord", but "between his shoulders" is just too much. Yet, "between his shoulders" has to mean something.

Let's see if we can dig it out. Shoulders…shoulders; they are a part of the human anatomy; this we know. Just a moment! Didn't we

38

have another part of the anatomy mentioned in one of our clues? Joseph's *head*! Our third clue (Genesis 49:26) was that "the blessings…shall be on the *head* of Joseph." Now we have two parts of the anatomy named in our clue search: *head* and *shoulders* - not much to go on, but at least they connect!

Even more difficult to handle is the concept of Benjamin *dwelling* between his shoulders. It doesn't make any literal sense for someone to *dwell* between someone's shoulders. Dwelling supposes a place, a dwelling place. How large would this place have to be? Well, the last numbering of Benjamin's tribe is listed in Numbers 26:41: "These are the sons of Benjamin after their families: and they that were numbered of them were forty and five thousand and six hundred." If the tribe of Benjamin was to dwell between shoulders, it would take some pretty broad shoulders!

The more we look at this the more apparent it becomes that "…between his shoulders" has to do with a portion of land, not a portion of someone's body. The word *"shoulders"* could only be a hint, a clue to the identification and location of the land that the tribe of Benjamin was about to inherit.

Let's go back, right here, to the question, *"whose shoulders?"* I don't think it accidental that verse twelve speaks of Benjamin and verse thirteen begins the explanation of Joseph's blessing. The twelve tribes are not listed for blessing in chronological order. I believe it will become apparent later that the continuity of verses twelve and thirteen have a deeper meaning than mere chance.

39

We know that Joseph and Benjamin were full brothers, the sons of Rachel. All of the other brothers were half brothers born of three separate mothers. Still, it appears that the connection of Joseph and Benjamin in the blessing order has a wiser design than the affection of brotherhood. Simply put, it is Joseph's shoulders that Benjamin is to *"dwell between."* "Ridiculous," you say! Smile on, for the meaning cometh. Ah, ah, just teasing, stay with me.

Joseph's Head Returns

Deuteronomy 33:13-16 describes Joseph's blessing in the new land.

> And of Joseph he said, Blessed of the Lord be his land, for the precious things of heaven, for the dew, and for the deep that coucheth beneath. And for the precious fruits brought forth by the sun, and for the precious things put forth by the moon. And for the chief things of the ancient mountains, and for the precious things of the lasting hills. And for the precious things of the earth and fulness thereof, and for the good will of him that dwelt in the bush: *let the blessing come upon the head of Joseph,* and upon the top of the head of him that was separated from his brethren.

The opening phrases of verse thirteen keep us in focus as we faithfully plod on: "And of Joseph he said, Blessed of the Lord be his land...." Joseph's *land* has been blessed by God. How can land be blessed? What is the difference between *"blessed"* and unblessed land? It seems to me that the only way to *bless* is to makes it rich, both on the surface and under the surface. It also seems to me that that is exactly what God did in his blessing of Joseph's land.

Let's take a look at these same verses in the New American Standard Version, as it makes it easier for us to understand this section:

> And of Joseph he said, Blessed of the Lord be his land, With the choice things of heaven, with the dew, and from the deep lying beneath, and with the choice yield of the sun, And with choice produce of the months. And with the best things of the ancient mountains, And with the choice things of the everlasting hills, And with the choice things of the earth and its fulness, And the favor of Him who dwelt in the bush. Let it come to the head of Joseph, And to the crown of the head of the one distinguished among his brothers.
>
> Deuteronomy 33:13-16 NASB

Here, as before, we are faced with the inescapable fact that the land is the key to our understanding the "blessing" of the treasure map. The hidden treasure we seek is not hidden in Israel as a people, or a culture, or a religion. It is hidden in the promised land, the tribal lands! The treasure is buried somewhere in the ground in the Promised Land. But that is hardly an "X" marking the *"dig here"* spot, is it? There is a lot of acreage in Israel. We must search for more definitive and exacting clues.

The Blessings of the Other Brothers

There are twelve tribal lands into which the Promised Land is divided. If we are convinced, and we are, that the *land* is a key, we must examine the tribal lands and their relationship to the Patriarch blessing of Genesis and Deuteronomy.

In Genesis 49, the chapter that deals with Jacob's blessing, all twelve of Jacob's sons are listed. Jacob addresses his sons and speaks to them in connection with their inheritance. For the eight tribes of Reuben, Simeon, Levi, Judah, Dan, Gad, Naphtali and Benjamin there was no mention of their tribal land being a blessing unto them. For Zebulun, Issachar, Joseph and possibly Asher the land is involved in the blessing.

We should notice the harsh words that Jacob has for Simeon and Levi:

> Simeon and Levi are brethren, instruments of cruelty are in their habitations. O my soul, come not thou into their secret; unto their assembly, mine honour, be not thou united: for in their anger they slew a man, and in their self will they digged down a wall. Cursed be their anger, for it was fierce; and their wrath, for it was cruel: I will divide them in Jacob, and scatter them in Israel.

Genesis 49:5-7

"Jacob's blessing" for Simeon and Levi are non-blessings, judgments. Later, we will see in Deuteronomy 33 that Moses doesn't even mention Simeon's name in his blessing. Levi's not allowed to

42

possess any tribal territory at all but Simeon will finally acquire tribal land.

Since Zebulun, Issachar, and Joseph, and possibly Asher are blessed by Jacob through their land, let's follow these four tribes in Deuteronomy 33 and Moses' blessing. Verse thirteen declares:

> And of Joseph he said, Blessed of the Lord be his land, for the precious things of heaven, for the dew, *and for the deep that coucheth beneath.*

"Blessings of the Deep that Lieth Under"

This is very much like Genesis 49:25 which promises "...and by the Almighty, who shall bless thee with blessings of heaven above, blessings of the deep that lieth under...." There is no doubt that "the deep that lieth under" and "the deep that coucheth beneath" are one and the same.

Because there was no technology to extract anything from *the deep* in the days of Jacob or Moses, neither they nor the children of Israel knew what it was that Joseph was inheriting. It is strong enough for us, however, to use as our fourth clue to lead us to the treasure of oil.

Verses fourteen and fifteen speak of blessings, but more of the variety that would be found on top of the ground, but Deuteronomy 33:16 is a different matter entirely. Look at the last half of the verse: "...let the blessing come upon the head of Joseph, and upon the top of the head of him that was separated from his

43

brethren." We have clue number five, or if you will, a confirmation of clue number three.

Another Hebrew Parallelism

The head of Joseph has indeed returned! It's not the only returnee, for the Hebrew parallelism presents itself once again also. Remember when we discussed Deuteronomy 32:13: "And he made him to suck honey out of the rock, and oil out of the flinty rock"? We have one verb, *"suck",* but two objects, *"honey"* and *"oil."* The action is the same and the objects *"honey"* and *"oil"* are the same, really synonyms. Hence, Hebrew parallelism.

Verse sixteen of chapter 33 has the same construction, a parallelism. "Let the blessing come upon the head of Joseph" parallels with "and upon the top of the head of him that was separated from his brethren."

This particular parallelism is much easier to identify than is the one in 32:13, yet is just as important to our treasure hunt. We have said that the first part of the parallel is usually symbolic and the last part is usually literal. Here, then, we have the symbolism of Joseph's head being anointed with oil by God. The next part of the parallel is much the same as the first, except it designates more precisely just where the blessing (oil) is to be found - *"the top of the head."* Not the back or the front or the side of the head, but the top is where the blessing is to be found.

A better translation of this word for *"top"* is *"crown."* The New American Standard Bible uses the word *"crown"* in this verse, as we noticed in the printed translation. Remember that the companion verse of Genesis 49:26 uses *"crown"* instead of *"top"* also. At the moment this does not appear to be very important, but later it will spring forth dramatically as a very necessary part of our map.

Joseph is Represented by His Two Sons

Perhaps you noticed that we left verse seventeen out of our scripture printout in both the King James Version and the New American Standard Bible. This was purposeful. The verse still applies to Joseph, but must be explained separately. The verse says:

> His glory is like the firstling of his bullock, and his horns are like the horns of unicorns: with them he shall push the people together to the ends of the earth: and they are the ten thousands of Ephraim, and they are the thousands of Manasseh.

This verse continues the description of Joseph's blessing, but is somewhat different from the preceding verses in that the blessing is transitioned to Ephraim and Manasseh, his two sons. "His glory is like the firstling of his bullock" is a poetic allusion to this very thing. Finally, the transition is made by the end of verse seventeen with "…and they are the ten thousands of Ephraim, and the thousands of Manasseh."

Jacob did not mention either Ephraim or Manasseh in his blessing in Genesis 49, but Moses here in Deuteronomy 33 has a little different situation. Jacob has already adopted his two grandsons in Genesis 48 so that they would receive Joseph's blessing when Israel returned to the land. Now that

Israel had returned to the land under the leadership of Moses, and he was perpetuating and defining Jacob's original blessing, it was necessary to use Joseph's name in conjunction with that of Ephraim and Manasseh.

There was to be no tribal land named "Joseph." Joseph would receive twice the inheritance of the other brothers, but it would be the names of his two sons that would identify the two portions. What we must understand from this moment on is that when we speak of Joseph in our hunt for the treasure, we will see Ephraim and Manasseh.

"Rejoice in Thy Going Out"

Jacob's fifth son was Issachar and his sixth son was Zebulun. Leah was the mother of both. As both boys were so close in birth and in life, it is fitting that they be close in their inheritance also. Deuteronomy 33:18 - 19 demonstrates this:

> And of Zebulun he said, Rejoice, Zebulun in thy going out; and Issachar, in thy tents. They shall call the people unto the mountain; there they shall offer sacrifices of righteousness; for they shall suck of the abundance of the seas, and of the treasures hid in the sand.

What we see immediately in verse nineteen are the last two phrases. Before we discuss what the verses are saying, let's notice that our friend the Hebrew parallelism has returned once more. In fact, it reminds us of the first parallel we considered (Deuteronomy 32:13), that speaks of sucking "*honey* out of the rock, and *oil* out of the flinty rock."

The same word, *"suck,"* is used in both verses. There was, of course, no word for *"pump"* in those days, as the idea and the technology for pumping was still thousands of years in the future. Yet, if we were to write these verses today we would say *"pump,"* not *"suck."*

The next question begs an answer. What is it that one could suck (pump) out of the seas and out of the sand? You don't pump fish out of the seas; they must be netted or hooked. Consider the sand. The idea is just as strange and difficult to comprehend. What in the world could be pumped out of the sand?

I think that the answer on both counts is the same: oil. In recent years offshore oil-drilling has become a normal activity. It looked a little different to begin with, but today seeing an oil rig standing in hundreds of fathoms of ocean water is commonplace. Sucking *"of the abundance of the seas"* is a *"last days"* phenomenon.

The sea and the sand, both known petroleum depositories, go together as closely as Zebulon and Issachar in giving us our next vital clue as to where the great treasure is buried. The descendants of Zebulon and Issachar, indeed, will have much to rejoice about.

Gad, of the Torn Arm

One of the strangest passages of scripture in the Bible is in Deuteronomy 33:20. Let's look at the whole verse:

> And of Gad he said, Blessed be he that enlargeth Gad: he dwelleth as a lion and teareth the arm with the crown of the head.

The last two phrases are certainly not literal, and they are much too strange to be symbolic, so they must be cryptic. If they are, they fit well with the anatomy code key that we previously introduced. We will talk more of this later, when it is time to decipher the code and apply the meaning. Take heart, patient treasure hunters, for the moment draweth nigh.

Asher Dips His Foot in Oil

Deuteronomy 33:24 is a very special verse for us:

And of Asher he said, Let Asher be blessed, with children; let him be acceptable to his brethren, *and let him dip his foot in oil.*

Here it is, as clear a verse to designate oil in Israel that you could ever ask for. Two things in this verse must not escape our notice. First, the anatomy code is continued: "and let him dip his foot in oil." Next, the word *"oil"* is used in such a way that we know that it couldn't mean olive oil. It has to mean petroleum.

Here someone might ask: "I agree that it couldn't be olive oil - that wouldn't make sense but don't you think that calling it petroleum is stretching the point a bit? If verse twenty-four was the only verse we had telling us of Asher's oil blessing, we could all ask that same question, but look at verse twenty-five! *"Thy shoes shall be iron and brass*; and as thy days, so shall thy strength be."* Aren't those first seven words marvelous, unique and thought-bending all at the same time? Asher has a foot that is to be *dipped in oil* and has shoes that are to be made of *brass and iron*!

Do you know that oil derricks are made of brass and iron? Brass against iron does not cause sparks as iron against iron does. So then, the combination of brass and iron is used so that sparks will not ignite an oil well fire!

A few years ago my wife and I were in Singapore. As we boarded the 747 to come home to Los Angeles, we noticed a large group of Americans in the ticket line with us. They were Texans, and they were friendly, but mostly they were happy to be going home.

As we talked with them on the plane we found out the most interesting story of why they were in Singapore. They had just flown into Singapore from Java, they told us, where they had extinguished a huge oil well fire. The fire had been so large and so complicated that the Javanese had been unable to put it out, and had sent for this special crew from Texas. Even then it had taken special equipment, three months of hard work, and thirty million dollars to extinguish the blaze!

It's no wonder that oil companies are so careful about sparks among the oil derricks. Isn't it amazing that Asher's shoes just happen to be made of *"iron"* and *"brass,"* the same metal combination we see used in oil derricks today?

The Fountain of Jacob

Deuteronomy 33:28 explains to us that:

Israel then shall dwell in safety alone: the fountain of Jacob shall be upon a land of corn and wine; also his heavens shall drop down dew.

This verse tells us three things that can be of help to us in our treasure hunt. The first partial sentence declares: "Israel then shall dwell in *safety* alone." The *"then,"* I imagine, speaks of the time that the treasure is found and the oil discovered. The phrase "...in safety alone" tells us that she will have no allies ready to protect her, yet she will be safe. This condition squares with Ezekiel 38. Israel's defense, her safety, is, as Ezekiel 38 so dramatically describes, only the Lord God.

The next phrase in Deuteronomy 33:28 is "...the fountain of Jacob." What is the fountain of Jacob? Is it the same as Joseph's well (many versions say *"fountain"*) in Genesis 49:22? Could it actually be an oil well, or even a great oil field?

Let's take the first question first. Is the fountain of Jacob in Deuteronomy 33:28 the same as Joseph's well in Genesis 49:22? The answer, I believe, is yes! Jacob's fountain and Joseph's well are one and the same for the following reasons.

(1) In Genesis 49 after Joseph's well is mentioned as part of the patriarchal blessing, verse 26 informs us that "The blessings of thy father have prevailed above the blessings of my progenitors...they shall be on the head of Joseph, and on the crown of the head of him..." The *"blessings"* of Jacob are to be found on the head of Joseph!

(2) Jacob's fountain "shall be upon a land of corn and wine" (Deuteronomy 33:28).

Joseph's blessings include: "…Blessed of the Lord be his land…" (verse 13); "And for the precious fruits brought forth by the sun…" (verse 14); "And for the precious things of the earth and fulness thereof…" (verse 16). Joseph's land would indeed be "a land of corn and wine."

(3) Jacob's fountain is to be upon a land where the "heavens shall drop down dew" (verse 28). The last of Joseph's blessings in verse 13 include "…for the dew…."

We may conclude, then, by biblical evidence, that Joseph's *"well"* and Jacob's *"fountain"* are one and the same.

Is Joseph Well an Oil Well?

The next question is a little more difficult, and the answer is much more difficult. Yet, it is there, buried deep in the sand of scriptural secrecy.

Is Joseph's *"well"*/Jacob's *"fountain"* an oil well, or even a great oil field? It is my belief and conclusion that, indeed, the latter is a biblical and physical fact.

This *"fountain"* is a great oil field yet to be discovered and developed. I am convinced that God buried this treasure deep in the heart of the "promised land" when "He divided unto the nations their inheritance." This treasure was buried (hidden) and not to be discovered until the "last days" (Genesis 49:1).

The timely discovery of this rich resource would "prolong your days in the land" (Deuteronomy 32:47).

It would provide Israel with a powerful position for this perplexing last days period. There would now be an overpowering magnetism in Israel for oil thirsty industrial nations. It is even conceivable that these parched national neighbors might come into Israel's front yard to seek a drink at Joseph well!

Breaking the Code

From the very beginning of our treasure hunt we have looked faithfully through our Bible treasure map for clues that might help us locate the elusive "X." After we find the "X" we will know where to dig. Meticulously we have searched out and listed each clue. Integrated with the clues were hidden meanings and cryptic symbols. As almost every clue referred to the land in some way, we concluded that the land was to be a key for our search.

Then we made a most important discovery: There was a cipher, a code woven in amongst the clues. We called it the anatomy code, for it utilized parts of the human body to symbolize or stand for location.

Let us briefly recap the code discovery. Joseph's head appeared first. The *"blessings"* were to be found on the *head* of Joseph, yea even upon his crown. Then Joseph's younger brother Benjamin enters the code. It was promised Benjamin that he would dwell safely *"between his shoulders."* We established that these were Joseph's shoulders. Then we came upon the strange passage that spoke of Gad *"tearing"* his arm with the *"crown of the head."* When we got the last anatomy code clue our imaginations just exploded.

Asher was going to *"dip his foot in oil"*! He was going to have shoes made of brass and iron!

We knew then that the anatomy code was indeed hiding a great oil discovery. We were sure that if we could break the code, we could find the oil! So, let's break it!

We know that the Promised Land and the anatomy code go hand in hand. They must! The context of scripture won't allow us to believe anything else. The code unlocks the secret that the land has held for millennia. Let's go together to the land.

We Find Joseph's Head

First of all we must locate the head of Joseph in the Promised Land. Remember that Joseph's name won't be attached to any tribal land in Canaan, but the land coming to Joseph would actually be a double portion. It now seems rather simple, doesn't it? If we cross over Jordan and find the tribal lands of Ephraim and Manasseh we will surely discover Joseph's head!

Let's look now at map #1. This map shows us the Promised Land. It also demarcates the land of each tribe. Notice how different each portion is from each of the others. It is apparent that the reason for the dividing of the land was not democratic or politically "fair." The "straight line method" used to divide states such as Colorado, Wyoming, and North and South Dakota was not used.

When you first took at the tribal distribution of land you wonder if anybody was responsible for planning who would settle where. Some tribes have large land holdings, while others are quite small. This is the view of the natural eye, the conclusion of the natural mind. But the division of the land into tribal units was not a natural project; it was a supernatural project. It was God, not man.

Map1

The Profile of Joseph's Head

Now look at map #2. This is the same as map #1 except the lands of Ephraim and Manasseh have been boldly outlined that they might stand out from their neighbors.

Look at the map closely. Do you see it? Do you

see Joseph's head? Imagine yourself standing behind Joseph. You are looking at his back. Joseph's head is turned to his left so that you can see a *profile* of his head. He is looking at the Mediterranean Sea. Do you see the crown on his head? Notice the Jordan River. It forms the back of Joseph head.

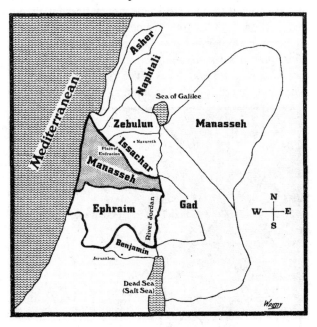

Map 2

There are two divisions as Manasseh forms the crown and Ephraim forms the head. Notice the classical styling of the nose as it follows the Mediterranean coastline. Follow on around as the line of the nose turns east, or right, to make the mouth and then the chin. Right here is a good place to say, "Wow

Jim, that sure looks like a head with a crown on it, but could it possibly be?"

Joseph's Shoulders

Let's see if we can confirm the conclusion that this is indeed Joseph head, and not a figment of our imagination. Do you remember the scripture concerning Benjamin? It is Deuteronomy 33:12, *"And of Benjamin he said, the beloved of the Lord...shall dwell between his shoulders."* We established that *"his shoulders"* were Joseph's shoulders.

Map 3

Look now at map #3. Do you see the tribe of

Benjamin? Benjamin is dwelling between Joseph's shoulders!

This is solid proof that the lines on the map that look like Joseph's head are in fact Joseph's head, for Benjamin is there exactly situated between Joseph's shoulders! Isn't our God amazing?

Now let us look closely at map #4. This map shows the tribe of Zebulun and Issachar outlined so that we see them clearly. Do you see where they are? They are situated side by side, but more importantly, they are both located on Joseph head!

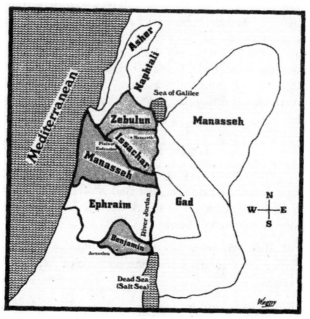

Map 4

From the very beginning we established that the *"blessing,"* the great oil discovery must be *on* Joseph's head. God had actually anointed his head with oil. Therefore any tribe, such as Zebulun or Issachar that has oil must be located on Joseph's head.

These two tribes according to Deuteronomy 33:19, "...shall suck of the abundance of the seas, and of treasures hid in the sand." Looking at the map we can see that Zebulun only touches the Sea of Galilee, and Issachar doesn't border on any sea.

Question - How can these two tribal lands provide "the abundance of the seas" if they aren't next to *"seas"*? The answer is easier than the question. If what is being sucked out of Zebulun and Issachar is oil, then the pool of oil is so big that it is "couched" beneath both the Sea of Galilee and the Mediterranean Sea! What a gigantic oil discovery that would be! Everything is fitting fine so far, isn't it?

Gad's Torn Arm

The tribe of Gad now draws our attention. Gad is not an oil-producing tribe, but Gad is useful in helping us with the anatomy code, as well as providing the position of Joseph's head.

Map #5 gives us the bold outline of Gad's territory. Notice that it is on the east side of the Jordan River.

Actually two and a half tribes held territory on the east of Jordan. Manasseh, because of her size, was given land on both sides of the Jordan. So then, we say that half of Manasseh's tribe is on each side of the river. Reuben and Gad were located entirely on the east side.

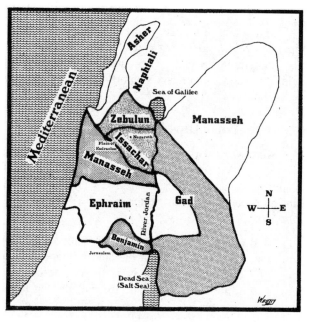

Map 5

Looking at map #5, observe that Gad has a long section of land that proceeds north following up the line of the Jordan River. This *"arm"* of land is *"torn"* by the jagged line of the Jordan. The crown of the head of Joseph actually tears the line of the arm of Gad's land.

Let's take another look at Deuteronomy 33:20: "And of Gad he said, Blessed be he that enlargeth Gad: he dwelleth as a lion, and teareth the arm with the crown of the head." The second phrase of the verse "...Blessed be he that enlargeth Gad" is speaking of Manasseh, for it is through Manasseh's natural land flow that the arm of Gad's land is extended (enlarged).

Manasseh, of course, is the *"crown of the head"* that *"teareth the arm"* of Gad's tribal territory. Isn't that something special? The anatomy code is even helpful to us in a secondary support!

Asher Dips His Foot in Oil!

And now for the really big one! Let's zero in on the tribe of Asher. Deuteronomy 33:24 says, "And of Asher he said, Let Asher be blessed with children; let him be acceptable to his brethren, and *let him dip his foot in oil.*"

Map 6 shows us the borders of Asher's land. As you look at it do you see that the land is shaped like a long leg? The top of the leg is north and the contour moves from north to south. The front of the leg faces the Mediterranean Sea to the west, while the back or calf of the leg borders Naphtali and Zebulun.

Isn't it just too amazing that Asher's foot, which is to be dipped in oil, is on the "head of Joseph, yea and on the crown of the head of him who was separate from his brethren" (Genesis 49:26)?

How much oil will Asher be dipping his foot into? It has to be an enormous field of petroleum, for the oil derricks will be so close that an airplane flight over Asher's foot would give the impression that he was wearing a shoe made of iron and brass (Deuteronomy 33:25).

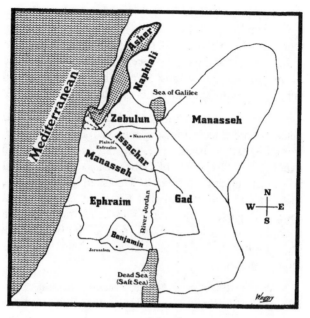

Map 6

What a dramatic and eloquent picture! The portion of land that looks like a foot, which is connected to the portion of land that looks like a leg, will dip into a pool of oil so enormous that it is beyond our imaginings. The foot will wear a shoe made of non-shoe material, iron and brass!

Wow! Genesis 49:20 will be fulfilled abundantly: "Out of Asher his bread shall be fat..." The word for fat in this verse is easily translated *"oil"*.

A "P.S." on Jacob's Blessing

We have discussed at great length the blessing that Jacob gave to his sons as he lay dying in Egypt. Our focus has been on the part of the blessing that had to do with oil and its discovery. There is another piece of information concerning Jacob's blessing that fits in very nicely with our study. Let me share it with you.

Turn your mind biblically back to the time and place where Jacob himself received the *"blessing"* from his father Isaac. The account is found in the twenty-seventh chapter of Genesis. Isaac was old and he was anticipating his death. He asked his oldest son, Esau to come in to him that he might ask of him a special request. Isaac wanted to taste fresh venison again before he died. Esau, the man of the field, was a great hunter, and he hastened to the hunt to do his father's bidding.

While Esau was gone, Jacob, having been informed of the situation by his mother, impersonated Esau and tricked his father into giving *him* the blessing (Jacob had already bartered Esau out of his birthright!).

"The Fatness of the Earth"

The first part of Isaac's blessing that he unknowingly gave to Jacob is the center of our attention. It is found in Genesis 27:28: "Therefore God give thee of the dew of heaven, and *the fatness of the earth...*" In the Hebrew this literally means *"the oil of the ground"*! Isn't that intriguing? But we are not through with this part of our story yet!

Esau comes back from the hunt to give his father the fresh venison and finds out that Jacob has bested him again. Verse thirty-four says: "And when Esau heard the word of his father (that Jacob had tricked him and the blessing would stand), he cried with a great and exceeding bitter cry, and said unto his father, Bless me, even me also, O my father." Esau continued to weep bitterly before his father, asking him if there wasn't some kind of blessing that Isaac might yet give him.

Verse thirty-nine gives us Isaac's answer: "...Behold, thy *dwelling* shall *be the fatness of the earth...*" (the oil of the ground). Isaac uses the same phrase, *"the fatness of the earth,"* both in Jacob's and in Esau's blessing. What does this show us about these two men, and more importantly, about the nations formed out of them?

Let's look at Esau first. Esau was renamed Edom because of his redness (Genesis 25:25-30). As you look at the map of the Middle East during the time of the dividing of the twelve tribes, you can see Edom (also Idumea) as a territory beginning at the Dead Sea and extending south in a fan shape. It was to be known as Arabia. Today Edom (Esau) is Arabia.

Isaac's blessing to Esau has been fulfilled for Esau is indeed *"dwelling"* on *"the fatness* (oil) *of the earth."* Who has more oil (fatness) than Arabia? At this writing the world must answer "nobody."

But praise God, we know differently! Jacob has more oil, a lot more oil, and one day the world will know it to the greater glory of God.

A note for you geology buffs: The Dead Sea is at the bottom of the earth rift (tear) that comes up through the Sinai. Tectonic forces could have actually squeezed the oil, like squeezing a toothpaste tube, down into Arabia. Wouldn't it be something if a latter-day earthquake in Arabia forced the oil (toothpaste) up the Jordan River (tube) fault line? It could go all the way up to the top of Joseph's head.

Let's Recap

Let us now briefly sum up to see *what* we have found, and *where* it is found. Jacob and Moses teamed up to bless the children of Israel with blessings that would help fulfill God's covenant with Abraham. The blessings were to be realized *after* Israel had possessed the land and divided it up into prescribed tribal territories. Some of the blessings were to be received a *long time* after the demarcation of the land (Genesis 49:1).

These *"last days"* that Jacob spoke of in Genesis 49:1 are the very days that we are living in now. We are now, and will be later, the eyewitnesses of the fulfillment of God's covenant with Abraham. This is especially important to born-again Christians who are in truth the "seed" of Abraham, and "heirs according to the promise" (Galatians 3:29).

When Will This Oil Be Found?

As I write these words, I know two things concerning this question. The first thing I know is that oil *has not* been discovered yet. The second thing I know is that oil *will be* discovered sometime in the years to come. The discovery could be at any time.

It is no secret that the modern state of Israel desperately needs Jacob's blessing right now. Her oil dependency on other nations makes her vulnerable both economically and militarily. With the international power blocs saying "no" to her oil needs, and a national inflation rate that is unmanageable, how many more years could it be?

What Will the Neighbors Say?

When the great oil fields that anoint Joseph's head *are* discovered, and the neighboring nations recognize the impact of the discovery, what will they say? What will they do? As far as the Arab nations are concerned, it won't make much difference what they say or do, as they are extremely bellicose anyway. However, there are other nations in that part of the world that would be extremely interested in a new oil field discovery.

The Russian bear, a near neighbor of Israel, is foraging even now for new *"earth honey"* in which to dip its hungry paw. The bear must feed her brood that guards her European hunting grounds. She hungers for *"honey"* and thirsts for blood.

Gog and Magog

Ezekiel thirty-eight begins with:

And the word of the Lord came unto me, saying, Son of man, set thy face against Gog, the land of Magog, the chief prince of Meschech and Tubal, and prophesy against

him. And say, Thus saith the Lord God;
Behold, I am against thee, O Gog, the chief
prince of Meshech and Tubal:

The line is drawn quickly and forcefully. God is
setting himself against Gog and Magog! There is no
doubt about the identification of Gog. It is Russia. If
you happen to be using an ASV, NASB or a Jerusalem
Bible translation instead of the King James Version,
you will see the word *"Rosh"* used in place of *"Gog."*

Magog speaks of some of the tribes or sub-nations
that have evolved from and with the chief prince of
Meshech (Moscow) and Tubal (Tobolsk). Russia is a
conglomerate of these sub-nations. Their original
springing forth can be traced all the way back to
Genesis 10:2. This verse gives us the Sons of Japheth,
who was a son of Noah. They are listed as: "The sons
of Japheth, Gomer and Magog, and Madal, and Javan,
and Tugal, and Meschech, and Tiras."

So, Russia and God will be literally at sword
point. Ezekiel thirty-eight, verse three says: "...I am
against thee, O Gog." We know that Russia has been
"against" God since 1917 and the communist
revolution. The great confrontation will finally take
place even as these verses go on to describe it:

And I will turn thee back, and put hooks into
thy jaws, and I will bring thee forth, and all
thine army, horses and horsemen, all of them
clothed with all sorts of armor, even a great
company with bucklers and shields, all of them
handling swords: Persia, Ethiopia, and Libya
with them; all of them with shield and helmet:

Ezekiel 38:4-5

Verse four tells us that God *himself* is going to bring about this great confrontation. "I will...put hooks into thy jaws, and I will bring thee forth..." The Russian bear will have *"hooks"* put into her jaws that she may be drawn southward into Israel.

What do you think these *"hooks"* will be? The word *hooks* is most certainly symbolic of something that has a drawing effect on Russia to bring her into this mighty confrontation. Do you think possibly that this *hook in the jaw* could be the newly-discovered oil fields of Israel?

It Is Only a Matter of Time

Analysts tell us that the Russian republics are in a state of diminishing returns. Part of this is attributable to the breaking up of the USSR into independent and separate smaller republics. Oil reserves are lower and have been kidnapped by inter-republic competition. If this scenario is correct, then it would seem feasible to think that Russia and some of her allies might consider the new oil fields an irresistible drawing attraction.

We see three of her allies in verse five. They are Persia (Iran), Ethiopia, and Libya. At this writing Iran has not aligned herself with Russia, but it is only a matter of time before she does. Since the tragic American hostage situation, Iran has little political or economic involvement with the United States in particular, or the West in general. Having been semi-industrialized and semi-modernized by the late Shah Pahlavi, she must ally herself with someone who can supply her with the industrial and military material to keep on going. Where she was almost completely supplied by the United States, she must now look for another "complete" supplier. Russia is the only viable candidate who stands ready to do that. So, as I said, it is only a matter of time.

Ethiopia is a Russian satellite state. For many years Ethiopia was pro-Western, but Soviet saturation has now set in. Libya is a country large in land, small in people, poor in agriculture and industry, and rich in oil. Libya has come under Russian influence also.

In 1974, Russia brought pressure to bear upon Colonel Moamar Gaddafi, the Libyan leader, to expel the Americans from their bases in Libya, charging them with being imperialists. As soon as the American "imperialists" moved out of the Libyan bases, the Russian imperialists moved in! That was in 1974.

In 1978, Russian and Cuban troops helped the "revolutionary army" bring Ethiopia in line with Russian communism. It was in 1979 that the American hostages were taken captive in Iran. They were released in 1981. The dates sort of move along together as if someone or something is orchestrating a concert for conflict.

The Last Days

Isn't it amazing how a biblical prophecy given in the sixth century before the birth of Christ demonstrates such definitive accuracy twenty centuries after his birth? It is a graphic demonstration for us that these are the *"last days,"* or as Ezekiel says, *"the latter years."*

I could not have written these words thirty-five years ago with any suggestion that these three countries would be in Russia's camp, for at that time there was not even a hint that they ever would be! Look at the years together: 1973 - Yom Kippur War and oil embargo, 1974 - Libya goes Russian, Ethiopia follows in 1978, 1979-81 Iran moved toward the hammer and sickle.

Yet these three nations are not the only allies of Russia that will move against Israel's "unwalled villages." Ezekiel 38:6 declares that "Gomer, and all his bands; the house of Togarmah of the north quarters, and all his band," will also be included in this great military campaign.

Gomer is the ancient name for Germany, while Togarmah is the ancient name for Turkey. East Germany, of course, had been Soviet-dominated since 1945. West and East Germany are now joined as one and will move in as a national unit - just as the singular name "Gomer" implies. There is no East Gomer and West Gomer! Turkey, like Iran, is situated on Russia's southern border, and will give way to her pressure.

What is the Time Table?

When will all this happen? When we consider the frequency of these recent dates, it appears as if it could be soon. Ezekiel 38:8 declares:

> After many days thou shalt be visited: in the latter years thou shalt come into the land that is brought back from the sword; and is gathered out of many people, against the mountains of

Israel, which have been always waste: but it is
brought forth out of the nations, and they shall
dwell safely all of them.

What an informative verse! It gives us five hints
as to when this huge military machine is to move into
Israel. First, it will be *"after many days."* The
prophetic day is a year, and so it reads more correctly
"after many years." This has already happened; many
years have passed.

Second, it is to be *"in the latter years."* If we
study Matthew twenty-four to give us the *"signs of the
times,"* we may conclude that we are now in the *"latter
years."*

Third, Russia and her allies are to come into a
"land that is brought back from the sword"!

Fourth, the nation is to be "gathered out of many
people." Israel, today, is exactly that: She is a new
nation literally "gathered out of many people."

Fifth, the enemy from the north is to descend
upon the "mountains of Israel, which have been always
waste…" This waste land was a result of the *"seven
times"* judgment spoken of in Leviticus 26:27-45.
Verse thirty-three sums it up briefly:

And I will scatter you among the heathen, and
will draw out a sword after you: and your land
shall be desolate, and your cities waste.

Israel's wasteland was a direct result of God's
judgment.

The Wastes Shall be Builded

On the other hand, God promised that he would reverse the process when he restored Israel. Ezekiel 36:6-11 is the declaration of this promise:

> Prophesy therefore concerning the land of Israel, and say unto the mountains, and to the hills, to the rivers, and to the valleys, Thus saith the Lord God; Behold, I have spoken in my jealousy and in my fury, because ye have borne the shame of the heathen: Therefore thus saith the Lord God; I have lifted up mine hand, Surely the heathen that are about you, they shall bear their shame. But ye, O mountains of Israel, ye shall shoot forth your branches, and yield your fruit to my people of Israel; for they are at hand to come. For, behold, I am for you, and I will turn unto you, and ye shall be tilled and sown: And I will multiply men upon you, all the house of Israel, even all of it: and the cities shall be inhabited, and the wastes shall be builded: And I will multiply upon you man and beast; and they shall increase and bring fruit: and I will settle you after your old estates, and will do better unto you than at your beginnings: and ye. shall know that I am the Lord.

"Thou Shalt Think an Evil Thought"

The five things that we have just mentioned are not in a future time frame. These conditions and situations already exist. The only thing that speaks of the future in Ezekiel 38:8 is the first sentence, "After many days thou shalt be visited: in the latter years..."

This refers to "Gog and Magog" being *"visited"* by the Lord God and drawn down into Israel toward Judgment. The next three verses, nine through eleven, describe the power and the malice of Gog:

> Thou shalt ascend and come like a storm, thou shalt be like a cloud to cover the land...at the same time shall things come into thy mind, and thou shalt think an evil thought: And thou shalt say, I will go up to the land of unwalled villages...to them that are at rest, that dwell safely...without walls...neither bars nor gates...

What is Gog's thinking at this point? What evil thought has come into his mind? Ezekiel 38:12 has the answer:

> To take a spoil, and to take a prey; to turn thine hand upon the desolate places that are now inhabited, and upon the people that are gathered out of the nations, which have gotten cattle and goods, that dwell in the midst of the land.

Look at the first four words of verse twelve: "To take a spoil..." Is it coincidental that the last three letters of *"spoil"* spell *"oil"*? It may or may not be prophetic, but it is interesting, isn't it?

It is inconceivable that this great invasion force would risk international repercussions for just "cattle and goods." Verse thirteen speaks of gold and silver, but this can't stand by itself either. If Gog was chiefly interested in cattle and goods, and silver and gold, then the attack would have to be directed against another country. Israel is not even moderately wealthy in these liquid assets. It would be like Little Red Riding Hood's wolf invading Mother Hubbard's cupboard.

But what if...? What if there is an enormous oil discovery "in the midst of the land"? Now that is a reason for an invasion of this magnitude! This would answer some of the questions that have arisen. Why would a community of nations as obviously gigantic as Russia need allies to invade a country as tiny as Israel? Why attack at this particular time? Why not use nuclear weapons instead of conventional weaponry?

At this moment we can only speculate what the *"evil thought"* of Gog's really is, that is, what the motivation behind it is to be. However, it is no secret what the heavenly reason is. It is disclosed in the sixteenth verse:

> And thou shalt come up against my people of Israel, as a cloud to cover the land; it shall be in the latter days, and I will bring thee against my land, that the heathen may know me, when I shall be sanctified in thee, O Gog, before their eyes.

The World Sees God's Holiness

The Lord God Jehovah is going to be sanctified before the entire world. Gog represents internationally-organized evil, and his defeat will represent the defeat of this internationally-organized evil.

The remainder of Ezekiel thirty describes the wrath and judgment of God on Gog and the allied invasion force. God uses both natural and supernatural weapons against Gog. The slaughter is indescribable.

Blood colors the mountains and covers the plain. Destruction is utter. "Defeat" can not describe the situation. Only one-sixth of the invasion force survives to limp home and testify to the power of Israel's God.

What About Armageddon?

As awful as the battle and destruction between Gog and God is, it is not the battle called Armageddon. Some feel that the battle of Gog is the first battle between God and the national world systems in the latter years.

Ezekiel 39:9 teaches that the weapons left on the battlefield by Gog's defeated armies will require seven years to burn. This figure offers speculation that the Gog invasion is the trigger for the seven-year tribulatory period spoken of by Daniel and John. Whether this is true or not remains to be seen, but the time of Armageddon's horror is fixed.

Revelation 16:16 tells us of this dramatic and apocalyptic battlefield. The word *"Armageddon"* means the *"Mountain of Megiddo."* In Old Testament times there was a city of Megiddo located on the *"great plain,"* or plain of Megiddo.

This historic battleground is located between the Galilean hills and the mountains of Israel. It was here that Barak defeated the Canaanites, and Gideon the Midianites.

The battle of Armageddon is really more of a war than a battle. Not only will soldiers be gathered at Megiddo, but also in the south and central parts of the

Holy Land. God declares that His sword "shall be bathed in heaven: behold it shall come down upon Idumea (Edom)…" (Isaiah 34:5).

Edom is in the south. Joel 3:2 tells us that it is in the valley of Jehoshaphat that God will gather the nations and plead for his people. Some experts feel that the valley of Jehoshaphat is in central Palestine somewhere between Jerusalem and the Jordan River. Revelation 14:20 says:

> And the winepress was trodden without the city, and blood came out of the winepress, even unto the horse bridles, by the space of a thousand and six hundred furlongs.

The blood will be five feet deep for the length of 200 miles! That is the approximate length of Israel today. This war of Armageddon will cover the entire land. Who is it that will be fighting in this terrible war?

Power Blocs of Nations

The Bible tells us that there are international power blocs, or groups of countries that will come against Israel. There are four of these groups, or power blocs, and they come from each direction of the compass.

The northern group contains Russia and her selected allies that we have already discussed in the context of Ezekiel 38. It appears that this battle begins the tribulation period. Although the Russian invasion seems to be part and parcel with this furious flurry of end-time battles, it is also treated separately in scripture.

Daniel chapter 2 tells us of the western confederacy that will move against Israel. It is a group of countries that will represent the old Roman Empire. Daniel, interpreting King Nebuchadnezzar's dream, calls this power bloc *"the fourth kingdom."* Daniel himself has a dream that is described for us in the seventh chapter of Daniel. It expands Nebuchadnezzar's dream. Daniel 7:7 explains:

> After this I saw in the night visions, and behold a fourth beast, dreadful and terrible, and strong exceedingly; and it had great iron teeth: it devoured and brake in pieces, and stamped the residue with the feet of it: and it was diverse from all the beasts that were before it; and it had ten horns.

The interpretation of this part of the dream is given in Daniel 7:23, 24:

> Thus he said, the fourth beast shall be the fourth kingdom upon earth, which shall be diverse from all kingdoms, and shall devour the whole earth, and shall tread it down, and break it in pieces. And the ten horns out of this kingdom are ten kings that shall arise: and another shall rise after them…

The Revived Roman Empire

As we noted, the fourth kingdom was the old Roman Empire, but the ten kings are ten countries that came *"out of the kingdom."* This *"revived"* Roman Empire is the power bloc that will come from the west.

There are those today who believe that this ten nation federation comes out of the European Common Market. The Common Market had its beginning on January 1, 1958, with the six countries of West Germany, Belgium, France, Italy, Holland and Luxembourg as charter members. The three nations of Great Britain, Ireland and Denmark were added on January 1, 1973. The tenth nation, Greece, was officially received into active membership on January 1, 1981. However, the number of members is still in ebb and flow.

Is the stage now set for the ten horns to fulfill prophecy? The Bible; teaches that three of these horns will be subdued by another who rises *"after."* He will proceed to take leadership of the entire confederacy, then move against the most High God. He will "speak great words against the most High, and shall wear out the saints of the most High..." (Daniel 7:25). Could the Common Market develop into this?

Yes, of course it could. There are those in Europe who have been looking for a superman kind of leader for years. Henri Spaak, an early Common Market leader, stated it graphically, perhaps prophetically. He announced:

> We do not want another committee, we have too many already. What we want is a man of sufficient stature to hold the allegiance of all people, and to lift us out of the economic morass into which we are sinking. Send us such a man and be he god or devil, we will receive him!

The Kings of the South and East

The *"king of the south"* heads the southern power bloc. Egypt is the leader, but there will undoubtedly be Arab countries in close alliance with her. Egypt, although oil poor, has been historically the leader of the Arab countries.

The fourth and last power bloc is what the Bible refers to as the *"kings of the east."* We can't say much about this, for the scripture only mentions it twice (Daniel 11:44 and Revelation 16:12). However, it seems that they must represent China, India and Japan, as well as other minor states.

The Whole Earth Is Against Zion!

It seems as if all four corners of the earth have been armed and are marching toward Zion! They come to represent by force their own economic interests. They come to do battle against any adversary that would keep them from their quest, their goal. They are prepared to do battle against each other, but then something turns their fury toward God and His people.

Christ's Triumphant Return

This is the time of the Lord's triumphant return in power and great glory. The military might of the world is aligned against him. The Beast and the False Prophet await the calamity of the coming Christ. John describes it in Revelation 19:

And I saw heaven opened, and behold a white horse; and he that sat upon him was called Faithful and True, and in righteousness he doth judge and make war. His eyes were as a flame of fire, and on his head were many crowns; and he had a name written, that no man knew, but he himself. And he was clothed with a vesture dipped in blood: and his name is called The Word of God. And the armies which were in heaven followed him upon white horses, clothed in fine linen, white and clean. And out of his mouth goeth a sharp sword, that with it he should smite the nations: and he shall rule them with a rod of iron: and he treadeth the winepress of the fierceness and wrath of Almighty God. And he hath on his vesture and on his thigh a name written, KING OF KINGS, AND LORD OF LORDS. And I saw an angel standing in the sun; and he cried with a loud voice, saying, to all the fowls that fly in the midst of heaven, Come and gather yourselves together unto the supper of the great God; That ye may eat the flesh of kings, and the flesh of captains, and the flesh of mighty men, and the flesh of horses, and of them that sit on them, and the flesh of all men, both free and bond, both small and great. And I saw the beast, and the kings of the earth, and their armies, gathered together to make war against him that sat on the horse, and against his army. And the beast was taken, and with him the false prophet that wrought miracles before him, with which he deceived them that had received the mark of the beast, and them that worshipped his image. These both were cast alive into a lake of fire burning with brimstone. And the remnant were slain with the sword of him that sat upon the horse, which sword proceeded out of his mouth: and all the fowls were filled with their flesh.

Why?

What was it that brought all these armies to this small, rather insignificant section of the earth's crust? For years I wrestled with this question. The battle of Armageddon didn't make sense. Why would the armies of the world be at that place, at that time, for that purpose? It seemed to be the wrong war, at the wrong time, for the wrong reason, at the wrong place.

In the natural realm it was. But God - he brings together all things to fulfill his supernatural promises, and involves natural conditions and situations. God knew at the beginning of days, alpha days, what would transpire at the end of days, omega days. He is the alpha and the omega. He is the beginner and the ender. He is the author and the finisher. He knew. He knew that man would eventually develop a technology that would require a gigantically perverse amount of energy to fuel it. He knew that oil would become the favorite fuel of "latter day" nations. He knew that the military and industrial might of each country would be dependent on each country's possession of oil. He knew that during the oil glut of the 1950's and 1960's man would squander a great portion of that earth honey. He knew that the Arab-Israeli war of 1973 would trigger the energy crisis, the petroleum polarization of the international body politic, and the greatest transfer of wealth in history.

He knew that by 1980 all industrial nations would be near hysteria, first for lack of oil, and then for the extortionary price of it. He knew that the kingdom of the world would be in conflict in the last days over this very issue. He knew where the greatest oil treasure in the world was buried, for He was the one who buried it. The treasure map, the great treasure hunt was His design. He knew where the mysterious "X" was all the time. HE KNEW!

For the latest news on the search for Israel's oil go to
http://oilinisrael.net

Other books by
James R. Spillman

- ➤ Omega Cometh
- ➤ Animal Church
- ➤ A Conspiracy of Angels
- ➤ The Fire of God
- ➤ The Resurrection Clock
- ➤ Parables of Light
- ➤ The Seven Israels
- ➤ Breaking the Treasure Code

Visit: *www.JimSpillmanMinistries.org*
for a full listing of resources available
from the works of James R. Spillman

About the Author

James R. Spillman

Jim Spillman, author, evangelist, and Christian educator was widely known for his charismatic ministry and personality. An ordained Conservative Baptist minister since 1960, Jim served in many churches of varied denominations and backgrounds. As an evangelist and author Jim used his unique mix of spiritual and educational depth with humor to reach people where they were. Audiences around the world were captivated by the power of God demonstrated in his life and brought to Christ for salvation, baptism, healing, and other mighty works of renewal. His background in education allowed him to develop a highly successful teaching style, enabling students to learn great volumes of material of the Word of God in a short length of time.

Jim possessed one of the largest personal libraries in the ministry with many thousands of volumes on the shelves of his converted barn library. The section on eschatology (end-times) alone has several hundred volumes. With undergraduate and graduate degrees in history and Greek, his library specializes in these subjects. Jim used this vast treasure as a resource for his writing.

Jim left this earth for his eternal home in late 2002. His work, however, continues to touch people's lives through books, and audio programs that remain as fresh and relevant today as when they were first produced. Jim's story and resources can be found at www.JimSpillmanMinistries.org.

The Great Treasure Hunt Continues:

Breaking the Treasure Code:
The Hunt for Israel's Oil

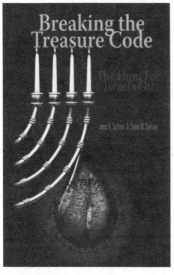

The story of Israel's biblical hunt for oil; **_Breaking the Treasure Code_** picks up where **_The Great Treasure Hunt_** left off.

What's happening right now? Who is involved in Israel's search for oil. What will be the consequences of discovering a vast oil reserve, buried deep beneath the *Promised Land*? Find out in **_Breaking the Treasure Code_**

Reviews:

"Israel? Proven reserves? Billions? When I read those words, the hair on the back of my neck stood up ... Little did I know."
Joel Rosenberg, _The Last Jihad_ series and _Epicenter_

"If you read one book on Israel in prophecy this year, pick this one."
Joseph Farah, World Net Daily

"'Breaking the Treasure Code' is both fascinating and relevant ..."
Jack Kinsella, The Omega Letter

"A substantial oil discovery in Israel would profoundly affect her future and surely send shock waves throughout the region."
U.S. Rep. Bob Inglis

Order extra copies
For your church or study group
*****

Breaking the Treasure Code:
The Hunt for Israel's Oil

- 1-5 copies @ $14.95 each
- 6-10 copies @ $11.95 each
- 11+ copies @ $8.95 each

The Great Treasure Hunt

- 1-5 copies @ $9.95 each
- 6-10 copies @ $7.95 each
- 11+ copies @ $5.95 each

Order online at: www.OilinIsrael.net

or e-mail requests to: info@tppress.com

or order by telephone: (864) 836-4111

or by fax: (864) 610-8047 *

* or by mail: True Potential Publishing
PO Box 904, Travelers Rest, SC 29690

* for mail and fax orders use form on next page

TRUE POTENTIAL PUBLISHING
the power of purpose

QUICK ORDER FORM

Description	Qty.	$ Total
The Great Treasure Hunt: 1-5 @ $9.95		
The Great Treasure Hunt: 6-10 @ $7.95		
The Great Treasure Hunt: 11+ @ $5.95		
Breaking the Treasure Code: The Hunt For Israel's Oil: 1-5 @ $14.95		
Breaking the Treasure Code: The Hunt For Israel's Oil: 6-10 @ $11.95		
Breaking the Treasure Code: The Hunt For Israel's Oil: 11+ @ $8.95		
The Great Treasure Hunt Audio CD by Jim Spillman @ $6.00		
Shipping: orders up to $25. add $5.00		
Shipping: orders up to $50. add $10.00		
Shipping: orders above $50. add $15.00		
Subtotal:		
Tax (SC Residents Only): 6%		
Total:		

Mail & fax orders please complete back of this form.

True Potential Publishing, Inc.
PO Box 904, Travelers Rest, SC 29690
http://www.tppress.com

TRUE POTENTIAL PUBLISHING
the power of purpose

QUICK ORDER FORM

Name: _____

Address: _____

_____

City: _____

State: _____   Zip: _____

Telephone: (_____) _____

E-mail: _____

Payment: ☐ Check   ☐ Visa   ☐ MasterCard

Card Number:

☐☐☐☐ ☐☐☐☐☐ ☐☐☐☐☐ ☐☐☐☐☐

Exp. date: Month: _____ Year: _____

Verification #: _____ (last 3 numbers on back of card)

Name on card: _____

True Potential Publishing, Inc.
PO Box 904, Travelers Rest, SC 29690
http://www.tppress.com